SUCCESS
FATHERS

James B. Stenson

Scepter Publishers
Princeton, NJ 08542

Nihil obstat:
Daniel V. Flynn, JCD
Censor librorum
Imprimatur:
Patrick J. Sheridan
Vicar-General
Archdiocese of New York

May 14, 1989

Books by James B. Stenson:

— *Upbringing: A Discussion Handbook for Parents of Young Children*

— *Lifeline: The Religious Upbringing of Your Children*

— *Preparing for Adolescence: Answers for Parents*

— *Preparing for Peer Pressure: A Guide for Parents of Young Children*

— *Successful Fathers*

— *Anchor: God's Promises of Hope to Parents*

— *Father, the Family Protector*

— *Compass: A Handbook on Parent Leadership*

Available from Scepter Publishers
(800) 322-8773 or www.scepterpublishers.org

Successful Fathers was originally published as Scepter Booklet No. 181/182.

© 1989 Scepter Publishers

This edition © 2001 Scepter Publishers
August 2008

Printed in the United States of America
ISBN 978-1-889334-37-0

Contents

U P UNTIL A FEW YEARS AGO, anyone browsing through the "parenting" or "child care" section of a bookstore might have noticed something peculiar. Though dozens of books devoted themselves to the mother-child relationship in children's upbringing, hardly any emphasized the role of the father. Among child-care experts, a father's enormously important influence on his children's lifelong strengths of character has been passed over and neglected.

This perspective is slowly changing. Over the past quarter-century, society has witnessed more and more young people emerging from childhood with serious problems deriving from weakness of character: immaturity and irresponsibility, alcohol and drug abuse, religious indifference, marital instability, divorce.

Professionals who deal with such troubled young people have long noted a common trait among them. Typically they have had a weak relationship of respect for their fathers. For one reason or another, their fathers did not exercise strong moral leadership during the formative years of childhood and young adolescence.

Increasingly, therefore, specialists have been studying the subtle but powerful ways by which fathers form their children's character, often unwittingly. They have also noted how broad social changes in Western life have seriously eroded this formative influence, leaving many children burdened in adulthood with weakness and uncertainty at the center of their lives.

It's clear, of course, that not all of today's families experience serious problems with their grown-up children. Even in our present social circumstances, many fathers continue to form their children's character successfully. Such men enjoy seeing their children grow up to become competent, confident, responsible men and women who live by Christian principles.

Why Do Some Succeed?

What are the differences here? Why do some fathers succeed while others fail in this critically important task? This book attempts to answer these questions, or at least to suggest some plausible explanations. It also considers some related issues that should interest any man who takes his fatherly responsibilities seriously: What are the natural dynamics by which fathers form their children's character and conscience? What social changes have eroded these dynamics, thus displacing the father's central role? What can a father do, once he's aware of the problem, to reassert the moral influence that his children badly need?

Before moving into a discussion of these issues, I would like to clarify three matters at the outset.

First, everything that follows here is the result of many people's personal experience and study. For almost 20 years I have worked as a teacher and school administrator, and I have long been interested in how fathers affect — or fail to affect — their children's character. A great many parents and young people have opened to me their own experiences and insights in this area. So, too, have I drawn from the work of many specialists: psychologists, teachers, marriage counselors and clergy. The opinions and conclusions expressed here, therefore, derive from much study into the dynamics of modern family life.

Over the years that I have spent in education, one impression has become increasingly clear. Fathers and mothers today, isolated as they are from their own parents and extended family, need as much experienced advice as they can get. Parents throughout history have always needed such advice. In our own era, however, they have to work harder to get it.

Our Focus

Secondly, throughout this book I seldom refer directly to the role of mothers in children's character formation. This I have done because of space limitations and, more importantly, my wish to highlight the father's role as clearly and strongly as possible. Emphatically, I have not intended to minimize the mother's crucial role. Far from it.

It has been the mothers, in fact, who have borne the burdensome consequences of the father's diminished role in the children's upbringing. The social changes affecting today's families have meant an ever-greater responsibility thrust onto the mothers. The ways in which they have coped with this increased work and worry have been inspiring and valiant. Society owes such women every measure of appreciation and gratitude for the immense good they have done.

Finally, I'd like to address a word directly to fathers: Men generally enjoy personal challenges. Few things make us more alive than facing complex problems to solve, situations that call forth our personal strengths — ingenuity, imagination, teamwork, experienced judgment, persistence, will power. Every day at work, we solve problems through the exercise of these strengths, and thereby we support our families.

The greatest challenge a man can face, by far, is that of raising his children well. Without exaggeration, it can be said that his success or failure at this constitutes his success or failure in life.

Many men, unfortunately, do not succeed in this venture. In the task of child-raising, as in professional life, no one sets out to be a failure. Falling short in this all-important responsibility seems to come mostly through unwitting neglect. In my experience, many fathers today are unaware that there *is* a problem — that, without intending it at all, they are failing to exercise the moral leadership that their families need. Why this is so, we will try to explain in the pages that follow.

You won't find any cut-and-dried recipe or detailed "quality-control specifications" for successful fatherhood in this book. There are no such things. Raising children who have strong character is, all things considered, an essentially mysterious process. And certainly no two families are exactly alike. Nevertheless, what we've done here is two things that should prove useful to you as a father. First, we've tried to clarify the components of the problem itself — what seems to be missing today, and therefore needed. Secondly, we've outlined what other men have tried and done successfully to raise their children well.

In our experience, this is what most men need in order to set effectively to work: a clear delineation of the problem at hand, and an understanding of other people's experience. When men see a problem as critically important, they bring forth all their powers of mind and will in order to turn things around, make them work, and solve the problem effectively.

We know many fathers who have done this — men who, with determined effort, have changed their ways and become much more effective fathers. Their experience forms part of our discussion here.

It's your children's long-term happiness that is at stake. What could be more important than this?

Character

We use the term "character" frequently in these pages, and it's a concept essential to our subject. How can we define it?

One point of view has proved especially useful. Character is simply the integration, into one personality, of several fundamental strengths of mind and will. These are internalized, habitual, permanent attitudes by which someone deals with life, in all its circumstances. They have sometimes been called the *virtues*: faith, hope, charity, prudence, justice, fortitude, and temperance. If these terms sound familiar, that's because you may have heard them in your childhood. For centuries they have described the ideal of Christian adulthood. Whether we call them virtues or simply strengths of character, they comprise the essence of what we admire most in people — strong character.

Though we don't usually use the terms, we do have a common-sense understanding of these virtues. We see them present or absent in people we know, including youngsters. Let's look at each of them briefly:

Faith: The active belief in God and in all that he has revealed about himself, his Church, his justice and mercy, the meaning of life here on earth and afterward in eternity.

Hope: The confidence that God will give us the means of salvation, and that his loving Providence watches over us throughout our lives; therefore, no problem is unendurable. (The Christian symbol for hope is the anchor — the link with God that holds us firm against the storms of life. A great many young people are desperate for this link today, and don't have it.)

Charity: An overriding love for God, a love that shapes and directs all other loves — for spouse, children, friends, strangers, material goods. In practical terms, it is the pre-eminent Christian virtue — a compassionate understanding for others that imitates God's love for us all.

Prudence: Today we call this "sound judgment" — the ability to make the important distinctions in life: right from wrong, truth from falsehood, fact from opinion, reason from emotion, the eternal from the transitory. It is simply level-headedness, the ability to recognize bosh when we see it. A well-formed conscience is part of this virtue.

Justice: This we would call "sense of responsibility" — giving others what is due to them. It is the sense of duty implicit in recognizing the rights of others, including the rights of God. In one sense, this consciousness of responsibility is the most important mark of moral adulthood — maturity *is* responsibility.

Fortitude: Personal toughness — that is, a willingness and ability to either solve difficulties or endure them. It is the power to overcome or withstand hardship, disappointment, inconvenience, pain. Its opposite (very common today) is escapism. Fortitude is essential to real love. Love, after all, is not just a bundle of sentiments; it is the capacity and willingness to embrace hardship for the sake of someone's welfare.

Temperance: This refers to self-control, self-discipline — a rational control over the passions and appetites, a self-imposed restraint for the sake of some higher good. Its opposite (also common today) is self-indulgence, an habitual pursuit of pleasure and comfort as ends in themselves.

When all of these virtues are integrated and internalized in a person's approach to life, he or she is said to have strong character. All other admirable traits in people (industriousness and piety and considerateness, for example) derive directly or indirectly from these virtues.

(One witty philosopher summed it up in another way: "Character is what you have left over if you go broke." It is the person himself minus his money and material possessions.)

How do young people acquire these strengths? Experience shows one thing clearly: They do not acquire them naturally or easily, and they certainly are not born with them. All of us, whether young or old, learn these virtues through years of practice in living them. We learn them by word of others and, even more crucially, by example. From earliest infancy, we acquire them by imitating people whose character we admire, principally our parents. Youngsters learn character mostly, and most deeply, from their mother and father.

If children do not learn these strengths from their parents, for whatever reason, they usually grow up without them. In one way or another, they are missing something important at the center of their lives. They retain the weakness of childhood; they remain self-centered, immature, irresponsible, self-indulgent, and without faith or confidence (in God or in themselves).

This leads us to the next consideration: How do the mother and father operate together, in different but overlapping ways, to inculcate these strengths of character?

Complementary Roles

What follows here is only a simple sketch of a highly complex and fundamentally mysterious process. Over the last couple of decades, psychologists and other specialists have probed different aspects of the dynamic at work between parents and children. As we mentioned earlier, they have focused increasingly on the father's role, an area of study that has been much neglected in the past.

The results of this work have been interesting and thought-provoking. Let's outline the principal features here, looking at three stages in a youngster's life:

Infancy: A new born child seems to have an initial reaction of fear toward his father. As he peeks over the shoulder of his mother (who constitutes his entire universe), he sees a large, deep-voiced stranger hanging about. Naturally, the infant is wary and uncertain how this intimidating figure fits into the warm relationship between himself and his mother. The mother, through her signals of affection for this stranger, signals the child that there is nothing to fear. On the contrary, this man is to be trusted, respected and loved.

For his part, the father underscores this trust by playing with the infant. It's a well-known fact that men have an almost irresistible urge to play vigorously with their small children: tickling them, bouncing them, whirling them in the air, making faces, anything to make the child smile and laugh. This seems to be an instinct to strengthen the bond between father and infant; it shows the child that Dad is both loving and powerful, a man of affection and competent strength.

Ages 2 to 11: Father and mother exercise different but complementary roles. In a well-balanced relationship, each parent carries out responsibilities for the family's general welfare. Though there is much overlapping, the responsibilities differ. In any event, the children see the parents respect each other's authority. What happens here is that the children develop an intuitive perception of each parent's general area of responsibility.

The mother's specialization is that of domestic order. It is she who organizes and exercises "quality control," as it were, over the home's operations. She is the principal force for attractiveness, stability, up-keep, order, harmony, peace. The appearance and efficiency of the home, its warmth and security, are what she provides as the acknowledged expert in these areas. The husband participates considerably here, of course, and lends his authority to hers in making the children cooperate. (That is, obey. Children's cooperativeness later in life seems to derive from seeing obedience as collaboration.)

The father's expertise and responsibility, on the other hand, lead outside the home. It is he who deals mostly with the world outside the front gate, the world at large. He supports the home by manipulating nature, by applying his mind and physique to material reality: by farming, hunting, handicraft, or some sort of skilled service. He is the one who deals with strangers in serious, as opposed to lightly social, matters: negotiating, contracting, dealing with people in a friendly but businesslike way. If these relations turn hostile, he stands ready to defend his family, by physical force if necessary. In any event, his attention draws naturally and necessarily to the universe of people and things beyond the confines of the home.

As we've said, there is (especially in very recent times) considerable overlapping in these two broad areas, and there are many exceptions to these generalizations. Nevertheless, a general pattern of character formation by each parent seems to be almost universally true of human families. Principally by example, the mother teaches order, attention to detail, steadfast emotional commitment, refinement, considerateness, patience. She is the force for stability and harmony. The father, also mainly by example, teaches long-range strategic planning, rational assessment of means and ends, courage, fair dealing with others, respect for lawful authority, and self-directed entrepreneurship. He is the force for purposeful activity, making one's way competently and confidently in the world.

How much of this dichotomy is learned behavior and how much of it derives from innate sex differences remains a controversial question, even among specialists. In any event, throughout Western history and in most of the world today, children seem to recognize (almost intuitively) that their mother and father have these different, complementary spheres of influence. And parents, too, have assumed them as a matter of natural course.

In homes where each parent respects the other's authority, the children grow to respect the authority of each parent proportionally. That is, the children come to adopt the mother's attitude toward her husband and their father's attitude toward his wife. A lack of respect, overt or implied, seems to undercut the children's respect significantly. A husband's neglect for his wife, a failure to support her authority, leads eventually toward the children's sass and disobedience at home.

Mutual Support

In homes where the parents exercise mutual support, the children seem to acquire a well-balanced personality. Along the way, to be sure, the parents must give frequent correction of attitudes and behavior: admonition, discussion, rewards and punishments, and the like. But essentially what happens is that the children unconsciously imitate the strengths that they see exercised by their parents — strengths that the parents recognize, appreciate and respect in each other.

It follows from this that, if the strengths are missing or if overt signs of respect are missing, then the children are left with little at home to imitate. This need to imitate becomes increasingly acute in early adolescence.

Adolescence: It's easy to forget today that the term "adolescent" once meant "young adult." By age 16, almost all young people acquire physical maturity; they have almost all the mental and physical powers of adulthood. Indeed, in most cultures up until the 20th century, people of this age were nearly prepared to leave home and strike out on their own. They were ready for independence.

The natural striving for independence we see in people aged 13 to 16, therefore, is entirely normal. What is pertinent to our discussion here, and often overlooked in our society, is how the father fits naturally into this dynamic.

As children enter adolescence, they want strongly (sometimes desperately) to learn how adults properly behave in the outside world. What is it like to be a self-reliant and strong man or woman? Where do adults draw the lines between right and wrong among themselves? What will my fellow adults think of me? How can I test my strengths and win acceptance among others? All these questions and related concerns swirl through the minds of teenagers. The young people seldom articulate their problems in these words, of course, but they search eagerly for the right answers.

To get them, they look increasingly to their father. As children grow into adolescence, they look ever more sharply at their father's attitude and behavior. In a short time, they will enter the outside world, where their father is the acknowledged expert. Therefore his criteria, his values and outlook, his judgment of right and wrong become increasingly important.

Psychologists have noted that much of the posturing and verbal defiance of adolescents is really a testing and questioning of their father's standards. It's really an attempt to draw out into the open, explicitly and clearly, the implicit and unspoken convictions resting in Dad's experienced mind: "Where do *we adults* draw the lines, Dad? You're the expert and I need your guidance now!"

It Needn't Be Traumatic

(By the way, contrary to widespread belief, adolescence need not be a tempestuous and traumatic experience for families. Parents who have exercised a steady, loving, and disciplined guidance among their children — especially in non-Western cultures — have very few serious problems with their adolescent children. Fathers who are conscious and confident of their authority fill these adolescent needs rather easily and undramatically; in fact, many fathers find that they draw even closer to their children as the youngsters approach adulthood. As we shall see below, it is extraneous forces at work in Western middle-class families that have come between fathers and their teenage children, leading to all sorts of problems.)

Apparently, it is not simply patterns of correct conduct that teenagers are looking for. What is happening here is much more important. Adolescents look to their father, more than ever before, to give final form to their *conscience*, the internalized objective standards of right and wrong, the standards adults try to live by in the sight of men and God. Psychology has substantiated that, though both parents must form the conscience in small children, the formational role gradually shifts to the father as the children approach maturity. Dad is increasingly seen as the arbiter and model for objective, unsentimental standards of morality. The conscience must be followed in the outside world, and this is Dad's territory.

Daughters' Model

There are other subtle forces at work here, too. Adolescent boys look to their father as a model of competent adult maleness. But, interestingly, daughters also look to their father — as a model for evaluating men. Unconsciously, adolescent girls and young women seem drawn toward suitors who resemble their fathers, or what they perceive their fathers to be. A remarkable number eventually marry men who compare favorably to their own fathers in personality, temperament, and character.

In the West, we have an interesting and charming social custom that is part of our marriage ceremony. The father of the bride leads his daughter by the arm down the aisle and then hands her to her betrothed. This small but significant act symbolizes what every father does with all his children over the years of adolescence: He bridges between the home and the outside world, leading forth his strong children to make it on their own. Both parents, mother and father, have given their children lifelong strengths of character and conscience; and thus their job is done. This is, after all, what family life — throughout history and around the world — is really all about.

The "Natural" Family

The psychological dynamics outlined in the previous pages have had to be somewhat universal and abstract. Perhaps we can concretize them by looking at what might be termed a "natural" family setting. What we are leading up to is the dynamic (sometimes destructive dynamics) at work in Western families today. The features of modern family life may stand out more clearly if they're contrasted with family life as it was lived in the past, even the rather recent past.

What follows is a composite description of a typical family in the Western world (the United States, Canada, Australia, Europe, much of Latin America) up until the early years of the 20th century. The description still holds true, we believe, for most of the non-Western world today — about 80% of the Earth's population.

We use the term "natural" here in the same sense that it has in describing any universally recurring phenomenon. The features of the natural family recur so frequently, throughout history and throughout most of the world today, that it seems reasonable to ascribe their origin to human nature itself — that is, to the dynamics among father, mother and children outlined above. We seem to be dealing with psychological constants inherent in parent child relationships.

What were the features of this natural family life? Let's describe them briefly:

1. *The home was essentially a small business, a place of work.* Father and Mother worked together as senior partners in an ongoing business enterprise, whether in farming, craftsmanship, trade or some other livelihood. The house was filled with tools and work implements, and the children constantly saw their parents at work, each in different but complementary responsibilities.

2. *The children played a low-level but necessary part in this enterprise.* Naturally the smallest children spent most of their time playing. The older children, however, did work that was needed around the house: chopping wood, drawing water, hauling materials, preparing meals from scratch every day, and the like. This work, being necessary, involved responsibility and therefore conveyed a sense of self-worth. (The long summer vacation that children enjoy today is a vestige of this era: the children's work at home was indispensable in the summer months.) Everyone in the family understood that the children's cooperation — that is, their obedience to their parents' direction — was essential, demanded, and expected.

3. *As children grew, they would take on increased levels of responsibility.* By early adolescence, they would be working alongside their parents in a personal apprenticeship, sharing in the day-to-day tasks of making the family work. A serious preoccupation with play and amusement would be a distant memory, something for the youngest brothers and sisters. These adolescents were more like adults than children, and they thought of themselves this way.

4. *Because cash and materials were scarce, everyone in the family had to wait for things, and to earn them.* Children thus acquired a sense of time and the relationship between effort and results. Living directly or indirectly off the land taught some truths about life: Some things have to be earned, some things can't be hurried, some things are inherently out of anyone's control. Relative poverty led to an appreciation of simple essentials: regular nourishment, warm shelter, good health, the confidence of being loved by family and friends. For everything else, the children learned to make do, or simply to do without.

5. *Practically every family had other adults, aside from the mother and father, associated with it:* grandparents, unmarried aunts or uncles, hired help, close friends of the family. Thus

children perceived a *range* of adult personalities and could thereby form a generalized concept of adulthood. Frequently the children could see these adults, by word and attitude, show respect for their parents; this reinforced the parents' authority and highlighted those traits worthy of emulation. Sometimes, in cases of conflict between parent and child, these other adults would support the parent's position: "Your father is right. You should listen to him." In a sense, the children were overpowered (and sometimes outnumbered) by adults who shared a common viewpoint of right and wrong. Adolescent rebellion could not get far against this wall of confident adult consensus.

6. *Conversation and reading were the principal ways in which young people learned about adult life and the world outside the family.* At home, recreation centered around talk — that is, the life of the mind. Story-telling, games, family history, Bible reading, friendly debates, discussion of issues and events — all this was the normal intake of children listening to their parents and the family's adult friends. A big threshold was crossed when older children were welcomed into this circle of discussion, having their opinions listened to and respected.

7. *Because future occupational positions were more-or-less fixed (and in any event the personal*

responsibility of the grown children themselves),
parents did not think overmuch about the
children's eventual careers. Rather, they thought
in terms of their children's future *character*.
Their efforts in the children's upbringing derived directly from a set of questions: Will the
children grow to be self-reliant, competent, responsible adults as soon as possible, before
they're out of their teens? Will they be honest,
level-headed, and honorable — bringing esteem
to our family? Will they live according to our
moral principles, and then pass these on to our
grandchildren? Will our daughters and sons
marry spouses who share our principles? Will
their marriages be stable, permanent, and
happy? Will our children remain chaste and
modest? Will every aspect of their courtship
and marriage remain worthy of our approval
— and God's? Can we count on the children to
honor and respect us in our old age?

8. *Finally, families were united in prayer and
religious conviction.* Children saw both parents
live according to God's word, trusting in his
merciful care. Since so much of life was peril-
ous and essentially out of control — through
sickness, accident, drought, famine, war — the
whole family was conscious of their depen-
dence on God. Prayer was important, necessary, habitual. It added spiritual strength to a
people who were strong already.

So much for this sketch of family life as our ancestors knew it for centuries. Note the dominant feature of this life as it affected the children's development: From earliest childhood, children were constantly schooled in personal strength of character. The children saw their parents as strong people. Every day, they witnessed their parents and other adults live the virtues: faith, hope, charity, sound judgment, responsibility, toughness and self-control. As the children grew older, they increasingly saw their father as a model of worldly competence, confidence and moral leadership.

The rise of industrialism and complex urban life in this past century altered this family structure considerably, of course. Fathers had to work away from home in blue-collar or clerical jobs. Mothers had to take on increased responsibility for the children's upbringing. New forms of communications — radio, films, mass education — exposed young people to alternative models of adult life, sometimes with values opposed to those of the parents.

Habits Remained Intact

Nevertheless, the formative habits of centuries remained reasonably intact in Western societies up until, say, the middle of the 20th century. Up to the period immediately follow-ing World War II (if we have to draw a line somewhere), the conscious task of parents in forming their children's character was seriously and effectively carried out. Despite industrial-ization, the father was still unquestionably a figure of strength and adult-level competence; he had no strong rivals for his children's re-spect. Children still learned adult values from conversation and from reading. The home was a place of social and intellectual activity; people talked, read, played, worked, and prayed to-gether. Limited financial resources meant that family members budgeted carefully, waited, earned, improvised, or learned to do without. The children respected adult authority and looked forward to exercising it themselves. Most importantly, parents still asked the same questions about their children's future charac-ter — and they acted to bring this character about.

We shouldn't romanticize about this by-gone era. Even then, modern families had significant problems. But by any reasonable standards, it seems safe to say that parental influence was much stronger and family life more stable than today. The divorce statistics alone would bear this out.

All things considered, it is encouraging that fathers and mothers in our modern era were able to raise their children well. Many parents are able to do this today. But the fact is that they have to work harder and more deliberately at the task than ever before. In today's society, such parents are a shrinking minority.

Let's turn to present circumstances and see why this is so.

As we mentioned at the outset of this study, a multitude of powerful changes in family life over the past several decades have seriously affected the formative, character-building relationship between parents and children. The traditional role of the father has been especially hard-hit.

Western Middle-Class Families Today

In the span of two full generations, two broad social developments have drastically altered family life. First is the unprecedented and ever-mounting level of prosperity enjoyed by the middle class. It's no exaggeration to say that our standard of living has greatly exceeded the wildest ambitions of material success that our forebears dreamed about at the turn of the last century. In a real sense, we have all become very rich. The second is the rise of mass electronic communications, which has introduced powerful images, ideas, values, and authority-figures into the life of the family. It may be said that the natural relationship between parents and children has been complicated by the presence of strangers in the home — entertainers, athletes, TV dramatic stars, news announcers, advertisers, and a host of other personalities.

These two developments have seriously altered the formative dynamics between parents and children. When we compare the situation today with that of the "natural" family, or even the modified natural family life of a few decades ago, the differences are striking. Let's look at some of these characteristics, paying special attention to the diminished role of the father.

1. *Middle-class children today almost never see their father work.* Dad leaves the house in the morning and arrives tired at night, often quite late. The children do not see him exercise his personal powers of mind and will while dealing with the outside world; they do not witness his character in action on the job, frequently under stress. They therefore lack his model of the virtues in action: discerning judgment, responsible control of events, personal toughness in solving problems, self-control in dealing with setbacks and difficulties.

When they do see Dad around the house, they generally see him at leisure — when his virtues are, so to speak, on idle. Even when he does do some manual work around the house (an increasingly rare occasion), this work is more like a leisure activity, a relatively enjoyable break from the pressures of his serious livelihood. The children seldom join in this work because they themselves are otherwise occupied with leisure activities of their own.

Increasingly, of course, the children do not see their mothers at work either. Pressures for a second income frequently keep Mom also out of the home and out of sight. Thus her own example of personal on-the-job strengths is diminished considerably.

What is left for the children to see, then? They see their parents mostly at rest, especially their father, and most especially with television. (One young boy put it succinctly to me: "My Dad mostly watches TV and just goofs around the house.") Unfortunately, serious strengths of character do not normally shine forth in leisurely amusements. And they never shine at all in front of the glowing tube.

2. *The home itself has become a place of play rather than work.* Whereas formerly tool and work implements abounded in the home, and toys and playthings were scarce, today the situation is reversed. Tools are tucked away out of sight, while playthings are everywhere: televi-

sion sets, VCR's, computers, stereos, electronic games, pool tables, dart boards, table games, sports equipment, and boxes of toys. (Typically, books are scarce.) These leisure devices, combined with soft furniture and efficient heating/air conditioning systems, make the modern home an exceedingly comfortable place. It has become an ideal ambiance within which the family's adults can relax and recreate their energies (which is where the word "recreation" derived its original meaning).

For the parents, this leisure is a welcome and necessary change of pace. But for the children — and this is our main point here — the surroundings of comfort and play are *the only world they know*. They have no spent energies to re-create. They have no strenuous tasks to relax from. Their entire universe of experience consists of comfort and amusement. Life is play.

A visitor from another century would be astonished, no doubt, at the consequent role-reversal in the modern family. In former times, the children would share in the adults' activities. Today the parents are given over to the children's preoccupations, which is principally amusement. Our time-traveler would see the home centered around child-like interests and activities. Perhaps it would seem to him that the children have won some kind of social revolution: the kids somehow run the home.

To look at it another way: In former times, the father and mother frequently came down to the children's level. But they did this to pull the kids up to their own. In today's family, by contrast, the parents seem to come down to the children's level . . . and stay there.

3. *Conversation with the father and other adults is minimal.*

If a father spent much time talking with his children about his life outside their experience — that is, his job and his personal history, his concerns and worries, his opinions and convictions — he could compensate considerably for his absence during most of the children's waking hours. The children would learn at least something about his character. Such father-children discussion was common until the invention of television.

But studies show that today this sort of learning happens far less often than most fathers imagine. Talk of any sort between fathers and children frequently totals less than 20 minutes a day. Really serious conversations, by which children learn about Dad's life and character, is extremely rare.

Some psychologists go so far as to say that outrageous behavior among many adolescents today is really a drastic attempt to capture, at long last, their father's serious attention. As we've noted before, professionals who work with troubled adolescents and young adults have long noted a striking trait these young people have in common: They know very little about their fathers, and they have little or no respect for them. During their most formative years, apparently their fathers never played a serious role in their moral development.

Increasing Isolation

If conversation with parents is minimal, that with other adults is even more sketchy. Typically grandparents live at some distance from the home. So do other close relatives. Neighbors are, at best, only superficial acquaintances; social visits are brief and infrequent. The family's relations with teachers and clergy are fleeting and far from the home. All of this separation leads to the parents' isolation from the support of other adults, and this has several serious consequences.

For one thing, the children no longer see close up a range of real-life grown-ups who can serve to round out their concept of adulthood. No outside adults are known well enough to reinforce and give depth to the parents' values (such as the children understand them). There is no one to show, by word or attitude, that the parents' judgments are worthy of respect. Thus the children have only one other source to form a vision of normal adult life: television.

Another consequence surfaces during the children's adolescence. As we've seen, adolescents have a natural tendency to challenge their parents' authority and values. Today few families have adult friends or close relatives who can mediate, as it were, the disputes between parents and teenagers. The children lack some outside adults who can explain the reasons and reasonableness of the parents' position: "Your mother and father are right about this, though they're temporarily upset. Why not wait till things cool down and then approach them . . .?" And the parents, for their part, lack adults who can give experienced advice and clear up their uncertainties. One of the most common anxieties of parents today, when dealing with adolescent children, is that they are uncertain whether they're doing the right thing: Where to draw the line between firmness and leniency? It is a certain amount of discipline too much or too little?

A Striking Contrast

Note how this isolation contrasts with the adolescents' social circumstances. Every day in high school, teenagers have intimate contact with dozens of energetic and more-or-less equally rebellious peers, whose solidarity in the teen-culture *ethos* gives support to aggressive defiance at home. Small wonder that so many parents in this position feel themselves outnumbered. Indeed, they are outnumbered.

We must note here, however, the one small group of outside adults who do have a significant effect on children. Male athletics coaches frequently serve as father figures for children, especially for boys. These men are, after all, the only adult males whom children witness up close in the act of working.

Boys see these men exercising strengths of character in the fulfillment of a responsible job: planning, discerning, overcoming obstacles and setbacks, dealing with disappointment, setting and meeting goals, competing honorably, working effectively with all sorts of difficult people and circumstances. The coach today fills the role that fathers formerly played in the "natural" family setting. He stands as a model of male accomplishment, and children are drawn to such leadership.

If the coach is also dedicated to the long-term welfare of his players (and the best coaches always are), he actively tries to form character in them, to build personal strengths of mind and will. For this concern, the children form a bond of deep affection and respect. Many adult men have lifelong gratitude and respect for the coaches who helped them so much in boyhood. Ironically, many children have more respect for their coach than they do for Dad at home.

4. *Older children and adolescents today functions as consumers, not producers.*

In most middle-class households, the children's active labor is not really necessary. It may be convenient, but it is not a genuinely needed contribution to the life of the family. Many parents, in fact, find it easier in the long run to do the children's chores themselves rather than nag incessantly. In such households, canny children can learn to evade work by a delaying action; sooner or later, the parents will give up and let the kids get on with their own business, which is amusement. Domestic peace is more important here than acquaintance with adult reality.

Families with tighter financial circumstances, however, continue to have a real need for the children's contributions. This is especially true of families with many children. Relative poverty means added work, as it always has, and this leads to real responsibility. Teachers have long noted that children from large or financially disadvantaged families generally show more initiative, reliability, and healthy self-confidence.

An Artificial
Leisure Class

What societal function, then, do most middle-class youngsters serve? It would seem that they mostly consume goods and services. Having plenty of time and disposable income, and a host of exciting new interests in adolescence, these young people constitute a substantial market for commercial exploitation. They have become, in effect, an artificial leisure class. Their only real usefulness to the economy is to spend money.

When they do eventually secure part-time jobs, it is often poignant to see the eagerness with which they set to work. The same thing happens when they work at a social-service project or volunteer their help during a civil emergency (collecting donated items for flood victims, for example). At last, somebody needs them. They have a chance to prove — perhaps above all to themselves — what strengths they really possess. In a sense, they are seeking respect, a genuine esteem based on adult-level assessment of their character. In former times, the conferring of this respect, and therefore the building of self-respect, came principally from Mom and Dad.

But even with part-time employment, the adolescents' life-circumstances remain those of child-like dependency. Though a 16-year-old has 95% of his adult height and weight, he cannot really support himself. He has most of the powers of adulthood with few of the responsibilities. For all practical purposes, he is still essentially a child and is expected to remain so (at least in economic dependency) for several more years. The lifetime habits of amusement, which in former ages dropped off sharply at puberty, now continue more-or-less intact until the early 20's, or even later. Meanwhile, their part-time employment provides "spending money." (Note the significance of this term.)

If one's outlook on life is formed largely through personal experience, we should not be surprised at the relentless pleasure-pursuit of so many young people. A substantial number of our young adults arrive at their 20's with almost no experience — either personal or vicarious — of productive, satisfying work. Instead, the preponderance of their experience has centered on leisure activity: play and entertainment. Small wonder they come to equate happiness with amusement.

5. Adult society, outside the family, also fails to make responsible demands of older children and adolescents.

The significant problems afflicting secondary-school education are too complex and controversial to explain here, but we can safely make at least one generalization: Compared with their counterparts of 30+ years ago, today's high-school students do not work as hard or learn as much about adult-level standards of professional performance. The documentation for this decline is mountainous.

Though the very brightest students in top-track courses still receive a reasonably rigorous intellectual challenge, most of the rest do not receive anything resembling an introduction to adult responsibility. Such an introduction, it would seem, is what school should be all about. Why else would we deliberately keep the most energetic part of our population out of the workplace, and at such expense? In so many aspects — in dress, comportment, work expectations — our large high schools seem like extensions of the elementary school ambiance rather than introductions to life as adults know it and enjoy it. To look at it another way: How many high school students, between class work and home assignments, actually put in an eight-hour day?

Eagerness to Work

Some critics have noted that teenagers actively seek part-time employment because they are eager to work for a change. Their natural need for a challenge is simply not being met in school. Even flipping hamburgers is more "grown up" than lifeless grammar-school-level instruction and work expectations. In the eyes of many teenagers, the high school ambiance seems determined to treat them like children, not to launch them into responsible adulthood.

Of course, there are great numbers of dedicated teachers who make serious demands on their students' abilities. These people consciously use high standards of performance to strengthen their students' powers of mind and will — to form their characters. Such teachers, like their counterparts in coaching, enjoy affectionate respect from their young people — if not right now, then later in life.

What about organized athletics for children? What effect do they have on character development? At the very least, of course, they induce bodily conditioning, and this is certainly preferable to stretching out in front of the television. But the point here is: What happens inside the child's mind and will?

Some critics have commented that belonging to a highly organized suburban sports league is like being a low-level employee in a huge, impersonal corporation. That is, you're expected to perform a well-defined function and you dare not make a mistake; beyond that, everything happening above you is an unknown entity. If this is true, then what (besides technical skill) are the children learning?

The sandlot pick-up games of yesteryear were, to be sure, woefully disorganized and filled with endless squabbling. To this extent, they were inefficient. But they belonged to the children. It was the youngsters themselves, with some occasional minimal direction by adults, who divided up sides, apportioned responsibilities, set and followed the rules of the game. All the apparently pointless squabbling, in fact, taught the children a lot about the way adult society works — conflict, discernment, personality assessment, compromise, fairness, agreement.

Note that adults then *directed* children's efforts but did not *manage* them. In terms of character-building there is a huge difference between these approaches.

An over-managed and under-directed set of activities seems to accomplish less for children than most parents imagine. If everything important is done for the children, including their physical transport from place to place, then how much do the children really learn about adult life, or about themselves? In our quest to keep them busy, do we direct them toward self-reliant responsibility — or merely away from boredom?

6. Television and the other entertainment media have become the principal means by which children form concepts of adult life.

The rise of television as an authority figure — diminishing or even replacing that of parents and other adults — has been one of the most subtle and significant social changes of the past several decades. Its effects are studied and documented.

As we have seen, it is natural for children and adolescents to imitate, mostly unconsciously, adults who serve as models of personal strength and accomplishment. For centuries, it was the father who filled this role. If the family had no father, then some other adult male served in his stead. (Such was the case with George Washington and his older brother, among other examples in history.)

But, as we've also seen, today's children seldom witness their father display his character strengths outside the home. Moreover, the children almost never see other adults show respect toward Dad. And finally, since TV-watching has practically eliminated serious conversation between Dad and his children (whereby the kids could learn of Dad and his strengths at least secondhand), the children are left with a weak overall picture of their father's character. Dad appears as a *relatively weak* individual: friendly, likable, leisure-oriented, somewhat dull, but not really deserving of high respect.

We use the term "relatively weak" here because, through television and the other entertainment media, children have a constant framework of comparison in assessing Dad's character. Every home with a much-used television presents children with an array of authoritative adult figures: musicians, dramatic actors and actresses, talk-show hosts, comedians and miscellaneous "celebrities." Studies have documented how these figures come to be accepted in the home, especially to children, as intimate family acquaintances. In many families, in fact, these professional entertainers are the only adult acquaintance that the family has. Many children know more about TV personalities than they do about their grandparents.

The key point is this: These people radiate a power (or rather an illusion of power) that overshadows, as it were, the children's perception of their father's strength of character. The entertainers seem to posses, in superabundance, those qualities that older children and adolescents long for. They appear confident, self-assured, supremely competent, socially and financially successful, popular and respected, sophisticated, brimming with unrestrained energy. They are thus, in effect, *rivals* for the children's respect and emulation.

Young people's attraction to these father substitutes may account for two curious phenomena in late 20th-century life.

Young People's Heroes

First is the strange assemblage of young people's heroes. When high-school and university students are polled about people whom they most admire, the result is an old mixture of personalities: Mother Theresa, Pope John Paul II, one or two prominent political figures, and then a collection of names from the entertainment and sports industries. Genuinely saintly people stand alongside politicians and assorted "celebrities." What on earth do these people have in common? It certainly isn't character. Perhaps it's simply that they all appear frequently on television.

The second phenomenon is the enormous influence, all out of proportion to their numbers, that entertainers have on the adolescent sub-culture. Though they comprise an infinitesimal percentage of our population, professional entertainers exercise a direct effect on the way young people talk, think, dress and behave. An extraordinary portion of adolescents' conversation deals with the doings and (perceived) character of singers, comedians, and other television personalities. Young people seldom talk seriously about any profession other than entertainment. When they do discuss other lines of work (law, medicine, law enforcement, business, etc.), their concepts reflect largely what they've seen dramatized on television.

Small wonder that such a sizeable proportion of young people display bewilderment, apprehension, and lack of realistic self-confidence when they reach full adulthood in their 20's or later. Since childhood, their images of adult life have been literally illusions. And their father, unwittingly, has done little to anchor them in reality. His own life has not given counterweight to the television's influence. Indeed, he has often been a quietly devoted part of the TV audience. Not much strength or effective direction can emanate from an armchair.

7. *Finally, the practice of religion is seldom a significant part of family life.*

Throughout history, periods of great prosperity have always seen a rapid decline in religious belief and practice. Perhaps this is because material riches crowd out the central realities of life — that we are all totally dependent on God, and that we answer to him for the way we live. Wealth gives us the illusion that we have life under control, and wealth's power diminishes our sense of ultimate responsibility.

Our Lord himself gives serious warnings to all of us about the dangers of riches. Surely it's a mistake to think that he was referring only to the tiny minority of the Roman Empire's upper classes. He was also addressing us. The Western middle-class of the late 20th century enjoys far greater power, security, comfort, and possessions than the wealthiest contemporaries of the Apostles. The abundance of our way of life exceeds the dreams of the Caesars.

What effect has this prosperity had on our family life? Among other things, it has meant significantly less prayer. A large percentage of our children hardly ever experience prayer in their lives at home. They almost never see their father pray.

A Concept of God

For very young children, the sight of their father showing deference to a Higher Power is important to their lifelong concept of God. If even Dad shows affection and respect to God, then God must be all-powerful indeed. He must be a Father himself — loving, protective, all-knowing, capable of doing everything.

As children grow older, their father's attitude toward God has deeper and more subtle effects. Psychologists have observed that the father (who appears, as we've noted, the "expert" on extra-familial affairs) exercises serious, and in a sense final, shape to the children's conscience — the internalized ethic, the firm judgment of right and wrong by which we live as adults. By his attitude and actions, he says in effect: "This is the correct way by which we adults comport ourselves in the world, whether we feel like it or not. This is the way we please God, our Father, and live honorably among other men and women."

Religious conviction is one of the greatest strengths in a person's life. It leads to many other personal strengths as well; it firms up judgment, purpose, confidence, and self-control. The children are looking for these things, eager for them. If they see this pre-eminent strength in their father, they are likely to adopt it themselves — if not now, then later. But if it's missing . . .

If it's missing, they will find other values elsewhere. Surrounded as they are by the allurements of a materialistic culture, they can swiftly adopt the rationalized life-outlook of modern materialism — that man is just a clever animal, life ends with death, morality is mere social convention, religion is a sham, life's purpose is the pursuit of pleasure and money and power.

In short, as children approach young adulthood, they face an existential choice: religious faith or materialist faith. That choice seems to depend enormously on the religious leadership of their father.

Successful Fathers Today

The changes outlined here have slowly and almost imperceptibly altered the formative relationship between fathers and their children. Over several decades, fathers have lost much of the moral leadership in the home, perhaps most of it. In our experience, most fathers remain unaware of this erosion and of its serious implications for their children's future happiness.

A great many fathers think they are adequately filling their fatherly role by simply providing for their family's comfort and then sharing in it. They're wrong. Unfortunately, they usually don't find out how wrong they are until their children are in high school, or even later when they're grown up and gone.

As we've seen, when children grow up without esteem for their father's strengths, they show weakness in their moral development. As adults, they are somehow out of balance — immature, irresolute, self-centered, irreligious, preoccupied with amusement and comfort. Though they may have gained marketable skills and a respectable income, their personal lives remain restless and unhappy. They have a 50–50 chance of winding up divorced. They sometimes desperately seek professional help, looking somewhere for the fatherly guidance that they've never known.

History has shown that children don't need comfort and convenience from Dad. What they really need, as a normal and natural necessity, is a living manly example of firm character and conscience — a man who shows them how to live the virtues we esteem most in people: religious conviction, active considerateness, critical discernment, serious and loving responsibility, mastery over oneself. The children need to sense, quietly and unconsciously, that their father is a hero.

Any father who seems a hero to his children is the object of their lifelong devotion. He is not remote and unapproachable, a severe authority-figure. On the contrary, he is his children's greatest friend, and unconsciously a model for all their other friendships. He is a source of happiness, confidence, humor and wisdom. The children's respect for him and his values serves to anchor their years of adolescence, to thwart peer-influences and the allurements of materialism. We must emphasize: This deep respect, like all respect in human affairs, derives from the perception of strength.

Even in today's prosperous circumstances, a great many fathers enjoy this respect from their children. They and their wives do an excellent job in raising their children. By definition, it may be said that successful parents are those who raise successful children. How this works is something of a mystery.

Some such fathers are active and outgoing, natural leaders at home and on the job. Others, including some of the most successful we know, are quiet and mild-mannered men, not the sort to stand out in a crowd. Some have obvious personal limitations; they are overweight or unathletic or medically handicapped. Regardless of their temperament or their personal shortcomings, they all share one thing in common: Their wives and children respect them deeply for their strength of character.

As we said at the outset of this essay, we have known hundreds of fathers from all sorts of backgrounds and family circumstances. Over the years, we've observed several traits in common among the most successful fathers we've known. With some variation in emphasis, the same approaches and attitudes seem to show up again and again in such families. For whatever these may be worth as experience, we would like to outline them here. As we go through each of them, please note how they approximate, in modern-day circumstances, the dynamics of the "natural" family that we've seen before.

1. *Successful fathers have a sense of supportive partnership with their wives.* They are neither domineering nor neglectful. They sincerely appreciate their wives' sacrifices, hard work, long hours, and loving attention to detail. What's even more to the point, they *show* this appreciation in front of their children. Consciously or otherwise, such a father draws the children's attention to their mother's outstanding qualities. He directs his children to share his gratitude and respect for Mom.

(Many fathers overlook an important fact of life: Men frequently receive signs of appreciation in their job circumstance — evaluations, raises, promotions, congratulations. But if wives who work full-time at home do not receive such signs of appreciation from their husbands, then they don't receive them at all. Children, of course, are innately ungrateful. If the father does not lead the children in this area, then the mother must sustain a heavy emotional burden, facing nothing but negative feedback. The children's respect for their parents must begin with the parents' respect for each other.)

2. *Successful fathers think long-term about their children's future character as grown-up*

men and women. They think of inner strengths, not career choices. They ask the same character-centered questions that parents have always pondered (the same questions we saw earlier), and then ask themselves: "What do my wife and I have to do *now* to raise our children toward responsible adulthood?" In other words, they see themselves raising adults, not children.

3. *As a consequence of this vision, they frequently talk with their wives about the children's character strengths and weaknesses.* Such men are conscious that their wives are probably more sensitive and insightful in these areas, and they respect their judgment. Though they may have disagreements with their wives on tactical matters, they are determined to come to some agreement; they realize how important it is for the children to see the parents united, especially in matters of discipline. Furthermore, though the parents may argue in front of the children, both are careful never to have a heated quarrel. There's much to be said for the children's seeing parental disagreements resolved amicably through compromise. But quarrels are a threat to family unit.

4. *These fathers frequently discuss things with their children.* Conversation is the most common leisure activity at home. Fathers talk

about their own childhood and family life, their job responsibilities, their courtship of Mom, their worries and concerns, their past mistakes and hilarious blunders, their relations with people whom they admire, their opinions and convictions, and so on through the range of their mind. They talk about grandparents, forebears and family honor. This does not mean that they bore their children or impose their viewpoints; sometimes the children (especially in early adolescence) don't want to talk at all. But they're patient and wait for an opening. As a result of this conversation, the children come to know their father's mind inside out. Over time, they come to respect his experience and judgment.

5. *And, of course, such fathers listen to their children as well.* They listen for what is unspoken and implied. They come to understand the changes taking place in the children's minds, and they steer the children's judgment about people and affairs. They respect the children's privacy. They praise them for their growth in character, showing their earnest expectations that the children will grow up to become great, honorable men and women — regardless of what they do for a living.

6. *Successful fathers keep television-watching to a minimum.* They realize that TV steals

time from the family's life together. It squelches conversation. Whenever something worthwhile is on, the family (or most of it) watches together. Otherwise the screen remains dark and the children constructively occupied: talking, playing games, reading, studying, making the most of the few years they will spend together as a family. Since curtailment of TV's "baby-sitting" functions means more work for Mom, then Dad pitches in to help. Under his leadership here, the home is more active, and consequently healthier.

7. *Successful fathers see discipline, not as punishment or mere behavior-control, but rather as a means of building the children's self-control.* They see that "No" is also a loving word. Without its loving application, the children may grow up with no sense of impulse control; in today's drug culture, this weakness could be seriously dangerous. From their long-range vision, such fathers realize that the children need practice and encouragement in overcoming their feelings now, so that later they will exercise mastery over themselves.

For this reason, such fathers do not hesitate to use reasonable physical punishment when necessary. We refer here to the minor and temporary pain that serves to underscore a serious lesson — in particular, the children's defiance of parental authority. Fathers realize that the children's long-term happiness is more important than the passing discomfort of a hard-learned lesson. In a short time, the tears dry up and the pain goes away; what remains is the line defining right from wrong — and this is what counts. When discipline is administered with love, it builds the children's respect and devotion for their parents. This respect, as we've noted, is the basis for everything else.

8. *Related to this, successful fathers are confident of their authority.* They know that fatherhood is not an elective office. Their authority as father does not come from the consent of the governed. It comes with the job; it comes from the responsibility given by God and taken on freely by the man himself. Consequently, successful fathers are not afraid of being temporarily unpopular. Their love for their children and their commitment to the children's long-term best interests — these are strong enough to override the kids' bruised feelings and their occasional reluctance to do the right thing.

In short, such fathers do not permit what they do not approve of. Though they may have inner doubts about the rightness of a given decision, they have no doubt whatever of their right to make a decision and to make it stick.

9. *Most successful fathers seem to have a number of close friends.* The home is open to guests: neighbors, relatives, colleagues from work, friends from childhood. Such men also go out of their way to befriend adults who deal closely with their children: clergy, teachers, coaches, parents of the kids' friends. Close friendship brings out the best in us, and it's healthy for the children to see this. The kids see Mom and Dad show the courtesy and respect that underlie all true friendship. Moreover, the children learn whom their parents respect, and why, and how they show this.

As the children grow toward adolescence, the parents have a network of experienced and supportive adults to rely upon for advice and encouragement. This support goes a long way in firming up the parents' judgment and confidence.

10. *Successful fathers frequently have a deep and active religious faith.* The children see them pray and take serious interest in doctrinal-moral formation.

This religious outlook seems to directly affect the way these fathers discipline their children. They are neither tyrannical nor permissive, for both of these extremes are basically self-centered. Their love for God and their family, along with their commitment to living by a well-formed conscience, makes them treat their children the way Gods treats us all — with firmness, understanding, and affection.

Such men are aware how their family's welfare depends upon God's loving care. The children's future lives are entirely in his hands. These men know that a lifelong habit of prayer is the greatest thing they can teach their children, and the kids' virtue of hope will provide an anchor for their young lives against any storms that lie ahead.

To look at it another way, these fathers know that every generation of children has to be missionized. Otherwise, they can easily lose their faith. The religious faith that has been a family patrimony for over a thousand years can completely disappear, can be snuffed out entirely, in just one generation. Today this is happening all around us. To any Christian father, the task of passing on this faith intact to his children is his pre-eminent responsibility. Nothing else comes close to it in importance.

11. *Successful fathers teach their children to be "poor in spirit."*

Such men know that excessive wealth can corrupt people, adults as well as children. It's one of the central lessons of history as well as our Christian faith. As the Scriptures say in many places, riches blind us to earthly and eternal realities. God did not create us to be mere "consumers."

How do fathers teach this spirit of poverty? In many ways. They work alongside their children at home, teaching the relationship between effort and results, along with the satisfaction of personal accomplishment. They are sparing in allowances. They make the children wait for things, and if possible, earn them. They give generously of time and money to the needy, and they encourage (but don't force) the children to do the same. They don't fill the home with expensive gadgets and amusements. They budget and save for the future, and thus teach the children an important lesson: Money is an instrument, a resource for the service of our loved ones and those in need. And that's all it is.

In a larger sense, both parents deliberately teach the children that real happiness doesn't come from pleasant amusements. It comes from other, more spiritual sources, confidence in God, a clean conscience, family solidarity, generosity to others, warm and respectful friendship, the satisfaction of a job well done. These are the real riches in life . . . even if you're broke.

12. *Finally, the most successful fathers always put their family's welfare ahead of their jobs.* They know that their children can be seriously hurt through fatherly neglect, and no job advantages — no raises or promotions or projects completed — can compensate for this loss.

Sad to say, it's common for many men to reach late middle-age or retirement and find disappointment in the results of their life's work. Some men work all their lives to build up a business or a practice, only to find that these accomplishments eventually disappear. Times change. New businesses and practices replace the old. New managers undo what others have done before them. No matter how we look at it, work can't be an end in itself.

But what about the children? They do endure forever, for their souls are immortal. The children's earthly and eternal happiness depends, in enormous measure, on their father's influence during the first two decades of life. This is a brief span of time, and it passes only once. God has ordained it as a central fact of existence: Parents have one chance — and only one — to raise their children right.

Successful fathers can turn in later life to enjoy the fruits of their sacrifices, their own successful children. They see their sons and daughters as confident, responsible men and women who live by their parents' principles. God commands all of us to honor our mother and father. The greatest honor that children can bestow is to adopt their parents' conscience and character.

To see one's children grow up this way is the great challenge and reward a man can have. It's what fatherhood is all about.

Questions for Reflection

A number of fathers we know have found it useful to reflect from time to time on how they are living their responsibilities as husband and father. We're all very busy at work and at home. Immersed as we are in detail, we can sometimes lose sight of the big picture, of what we're after in the long run. As is true in business, we sometimes need to step back and question what we're really doing, and why.

The questions below form a sort of self-examination that successful fathers have used to stay on top of things. We hope that some or all of them may prove useful to you.

1. Given the many forces acting on the formation of my children's character, how often do I think seriously about what strengths of character they see in me — in the way I habitually live faith, hope, charity, sound judgment, a sense of responsibility, personal toughness, and self-discipline? If they don't see these strengths in *me*, where *will* they see them? If I'm not a leader to them, then who is?

2. Where, in their daily lives, do the kids see attractive examples of the *opposites* of these virtues: religious indifference and materialism, despair and self-doubt, selfishness, sloppy

thinking (especially about moral issues), immaturity and irresponsibility, softness, self-indulgence?

3. If the young children already show signs of these character weaknesses, what will they be like in their teens and early 20's? How could these weaknesses affect the stability and happiness of their marriage? Are they headed for trouble?

4. How much do the children know about my work? Do they understand how I have to exercise strength of character in earning a living — in approaching and overcoming problems, in handling obstacles and setbacks, in dealing with tight deadlines and difficult people, in improvising and doing without? Do they grasp *how* and *why* I derive personal satisfaction from my work? (Or, on the other hand, do they think enjoyment comes mainly from leisure and amusements?)

5. Whom do the children respect and admire, and why? Whom did I respect and admire when I was their age? Do the children know whom I esteem *now*, and why?

6. In what circumstances do the children see me show respect for others — in religious prac-

tice, in public courtesy and good manners, in our conversation about people at home? What could happen to the kids later if they grow up without an habitual respect for the rights of others, starting with God?

7. Do the children show enough respect and appreciation for their mother? Under what circumstances do they see *me* display my gratitude, appreciation, and deep respect for her?

8. Are the kids fully aware that their mother is the #1 person in my life? What do I say and do to draw their attention to their mother's outstanding character and admirable qualities? Do I show my daughters that their mother is, in my estimation, a model for the kind of woman they should grow to become? Are my sons aware that their mother is a model for what they should seek in their future wife?

9. Is there a sense of "family honor" and "family name" among our children? How much do the children know about our family's history? Do the kids know much about the lives of their grandparents — their struggles and quiet courage, their adherence to our religious and cultural values (passed on now to yet another generation), their worthiness of respect, affection, and gratitude?

10. How many hours of television do the children watch each week? How much of the "television culture" can be seen in their interests and conversation? What sort of television personalities do they admire?

11. What could the children be *learning* if their TV time went into other activities: reading, music lessons, puzzles, working with their hands, visiting the elderly, interacting with different types of people, planning and executing projects, helping to organize and carry out family activities? In what way would they thus be stronger, more mature, more self-reliant and responsible? (In other words, what are they missing by watching so much television?)

12. If the television stops functioning as a baby-sitter at home, how can I help my wife with the increased responsibility of keeping the kids' minds constructively occupied? In what ways would my bond with the children grow stronger?

13. Are the children's sports activities over-managed by adults — thus inducing active bodies but passive minds? Are the kids' coaches teaching anything besides technical skill? What are the children learning about fairness, persistence, honorable competition, getting along

with different types of people, appreciating people's earnest efforts and good intentions? How can I contribute to this character-building dimension of athletics?

14. Do I occasionally remind myself that the children (the older ones especially) unconsciously *compare* my character to that of other people: peers, coaches, teachers, rock stars, entertainers, and other adults who enter their lives? Do they perceive me as relatively stodgy, passive, dull, set in my ways — and therefore weak? Or do they see me as strong, self-confident, principled, fair-minded, discriminating, open to new interests, willing to improve myself and strengthen my character? To whom do the kids look for a model for adult-level strength and competence — to me, or to celebrities of the entertainment or sports industries.

15. Am I able to "get down to the kids' level" — to see life as they see it? But am I careful not to *stay* there? Do I *lift them up,* so to speak, *to my level* — to help them see life as adults see it? Do the kids see men, in other words, *enjoying* the challenges of family life and living as a responsible adult?

16. Do the kids see that I am proud and honored by the strengths of character that I see growing inside them?

Index

Personal Notes